10 Things I Wish My Mother Taught Me About $$$

Gen Zs Guide to Financial and Personal Bliss

By

Dovév Weaver Sr

Disclaimer

The views and opinions expressed in this book are those of the author's alone and do not necessarily reflect the official policy or position of any agency of Amazon.com or its affiliates. The content of this book is provided for informational and entertainment purposes only and should not be construed as professional advice.

The accuracy and completeness of the information provided herein are not guaranteed or warranted to produce any particular results, and the advice and strategies contained herein may not be suitable for every individual. Neither the publisher nor the author shall be liable for any loss of profit or any other commercial damages, including but not limited to special, incidental, consequential, or other damages.

Connect with Coach D

Stay connected and be inspired by following Coach D on social media! Join our vibrant online community where you can gain valuable insights, motivation, and support on your journey to manifesting your dreams. Follow Coach D on all social media platforms for the latest updates, inspirational content, and interactive engagement.

Follow Coach D on Social Media

- **Instagram:** @coachdtalks
- **Facebook:** @coachdtalks
- **YouTube:** @coachdtalks

Why Connect with Coach D?

- **Daily Inspiration:** Get daily doses of motivation and positivity to keep you on track with your goals.
- **Expert Advice:** Access valuable tips and strategies on personal development, goal setting, and achieving success.
- **Community Support:** Join a community of like-minded individuals who are also on their journey to manifesting their dreams.

- **Interactive Content:** Participate in live sessions, Q&A segments, and discussions that will help you stay engaged and focused.

Be Part of the Journey

Connecting with Coach D online means you are never alone on your path to success. Engage with content that resonates, ask questions, share your progress, and celebrate your achievements with a supportive community.

Don't miss out on the opportunity to transform your life. Follow Coach D on your favorite social media platforms today!

Stay inspired, stay motivated, and let's manifest those dreams together!

Dedication:

I would like to dedicate this book to my grandfather Neavel T. Weaver. I found out later in my life that he was an entrepreneur himself up north and he had his own dry cleaning business where they delivered pressed clothes to their customers in the city. Finding out he was an entrepreneur has inspired me to not only teach my kids about Entrepreneurship but all the kids in the world about business ownership. It is not easy, but it is worth it. My mother and I will be launching a Non-Profit called The Neavel T Weaver Foundation in the near future and we are going to teach kids about entrepreneurship, financial literacy, mental health, Christian values and leadership development. Granddad I pray that you are proud of me and I hope you will continue to be my guiding light as I continue on this journey of Entrepreneurship.

Table OF Contents

INTRODUCTION 1
The Magic Of Money 1
Why Money Matters 2
A Treasure Map For Your Pocket 3

Chapter 1 12

THE FIRST COIN 4
What Money Is And Where It Comes From 4
Earning Your Gold - Chores And Allowance 8
Saving In Your Piggy Bank 12

Chapter 2 26

MY MONEY, YOUR MONEY 18
Learning To Share And Spend 18
The Joy Of Giving - Birthdays And Holidays 21
Understanding Needs Vs. Wants 24

Chapter 3 37

THE QUEST FOR MORE COINS 29
Ways To Earn Money As A Kid 29
Lemonade Stands And Garage Sales 33
Being A Young Entrepreneur 37

Chapter 4 49

GUARDING THE TREASURE CHEST 41
Starting Your Savings Adventure 41
Goals And Wishes - Saving For Something Big 44
The Patience Game - Waiting For What You Want 47

Chapter 5 59

MONEY WIZARDS AND THEIR SECRETS 53
Banks: The Caves Where Money Wizards Keep Your Coins Safe 53
Interest: The Spell That Grows Your Money 57

When The Money Wizard Needs Their Coins Back - Borrowing And Returning....60

Chapter 6 74

THE MARKETPLACE MAZE....66
Smart Shopping With Mom....66
Coupons And Sales - The Quest For Bargains....69
The Enchanted Objects - Advertising And Its Tricks....74

Chapter 7 86

THE TREASURE MAP REDRAWN....78
Budgeting: Planning Your Spending Adventure....78
The Four Coin Jars - Save, Spend, Donate, Invest....80
Keeping Track Of Your Coins....83

Chapter 8 94

THE FUTURE TREASURE HUNT....86
Dreams Of The Future - Why It's Never Too Early To Save....86
Planting The Seeds - Investing In Your Future....88
Sharing The Wealth - Why Giving Can Make You Happy....90
CONCLUSION....93

Introduction

This isn't just a book; it's your roadmap to understanding how money works and how you can manage it to make your dreams come true. From the coins jingling in your pocket to the notes you save in your piggy bank, each piece of money tells a story and holds the key to new possibilities. Let's start exploring this amazing world together!

The Magic of Money

Have you ever wondered why money feels so important? It's because money is like a tool—a very special kind of tool that can help you buy things you need and want, help others, and even save up for something big in the future.

Money is powerful because it is universally accepted in exchange for goods and services. Imagine trying to buy a chocolate bar with a drawing you made. It might work at home, but in a store, money is what you need.

Money also acts as a way to keep score. It helps people decide the value of things. How much is a new video game worth? How about an hour of mowing the lawn? Money helps everyone agree on answers to these questions. It is a magic that is woven into every part of our lives, from buying a morning snack to saving up for a new bike.

Why Money Matters

Understanding money is important because it affects nearly every part of our lives. Knowing how to manage money wisely can make life a lot smoother and more fun. It can help you get things you need, like clothes and food, while also saving for things you really want, like a new toy or a trip to an amusement park. Being smart with money means you can handle surprises, like if something breaks and needs to be fixed.

Money also helps you learn how to make good decisions. When you think about what you really need versus what you just want for fun, you are learning to set priorities and plan ahead. These are skills that will help you all through life, no matter what you do or where you go.

A Treasure Map for Your Pocket

This book is like a treasure map. It will show you paths and shortcuts to help you make the most of your money. You will learn how to earn money by doing chores or selling things you no longer need. You will discover the best ways to save, whether it's in a piggy bank at home or a savings account at a bank. And you'll find out how spending money wisely can be just as important as saving it.

Along the way, you'll meet people who know a lot about money—like bankers and store owners—and learn from their experiences. You'll see how money can grow if you're patient, and learn why sometimes it's smart to wait before buying something you want.

Chapter 1

The First Coin

What Money Is and Where It Comes From

Here, we'll explore the basics: what money actually is and where it comes from. This might sound simple, but understanding these concepts is the first big step in becoming smart about handling your finances.

What is Money?

Money is something that people use to pay for goods and services. Throughout history, many things have been used as money, from shells and grains to the coins and paper bills we use today. The most important thing about money is that everyone must agree on its value. It doesn't matter what it's made of—as long as everyone in an economy agrees to accept it in exchange for goods and services, it can function as money.

Today, most countries have their own type of money, such as dollars, euros, or yen. Each type of money is a unit of exchange that can be broken down into smaller parts (like cents), which helps in buying cheaper items or giving exact change.

Where Does Money Come From?

Minting and Printing

Money comes into existence in different ways. Coins are usually made at a place called a mint. Mints are special factories where metals are stamped into coins, with specific designs that often feature important symbols or leaders from a country. Paper money, on the other hand, is printed in secure facilities. These facilities ensure that the money is tough to copy, using special paper, inks, and designs that are hard to fake.

Banks and Digital Money

While physical money is made at mints and printing facilities, digital money is a bit different.

When you deposit money in a bank, it becomes part of the bank's electronic records. Most of the money in the world today actually exists as numbers in computers rather than as actual pieces of paper or metal. This digital money can be moved, spent, and saved without ever turning into physical cash.

Government Role

Governments and central banks play a huge role in creating money and managing its supply. They decide how much new money to print and release into the economy, which can affect everything from how much things cost to how easy it is to get a job.

How Money Gains Value

Money has value because people agree to give it value. This agreement is a kind of promise. It's like everyone in a community making a promise that they will accept money in exchange for things like food, clothes, toys, or services like haircuts.

The value of money can change, though. If a government makes too much money, it can become less valuable. This is called inflation. When inflation happens, it takes more money to buy the same things as before. That's why governments must be careful about how much new money they create.

The Journey of a Coin

Imagine a single coin, like the one you might find under the couch cushions. This coin could have been in hundreds of pockets, used to buy anything from a piece of candy to a ride on a bus. It gets passed around from person to person, traveling much farther than you might think.

Every coin tells a story. It could have been part of someone's first allowance, or used in a city far away. By the time it reaches your hand, that coin has likely been part of many people's lives, helping them in small but important ways. That's the beauty of money—it connects us to a larger story, one that includes everyone who's ever used that piece of money.

Earning Your Gold - Chores and Allowance

As you begin your journey into the world of money, one of the first steps you'll take is earning your own money. For many kids, this starts with chores and an allowance. These are not just ways to earn some cash; they are your first lessons in responsibility and the value of hard work.

What is an Allowance?

An allowance is a small amount of money given to you by your parents or guardians, usually every week or month. The idea behind an allowance is to teach you how to manage money responsibly. With an allowance, you can learn to budget, save, and make decisions about spending money. It's like training wheels for managing finances when you grow up.

Why Do Chores Matter?

Chores are tasks or jobs that you do around the house to help your family. These might include tidying up your room, doing the dishes, taking out the trash, or helping to care for pets. When you do chores, you contribute to your home and learn valuable skills. It's not just about cleaning or organizing; it's about becoming a responsible part of your family and learning teamwork.

Earning Money Through Chores

Many families link chores to an allowance as a way to earn money. This system can work in different ways:

Fixed Allowance

You get a set amount of money regularly, no matter what chores you do.

Pay Per Chore

You earn money for each chore you complete.

Bonus for Extra Tasks

You might get a regular allowance, but can earn extra by doing additional tasks beyond your usual chores.

This setup teaches you that money must be earned and gives you a sense of achievement when you receive your allowance. It also starts to teach you about the world of work, where people are paid for their labour.

Managing Your First Earnings

Once you start earning money, you face decisions about what to do with it. Here's where you learn to set priorities. Do you spend it right away on something fun? Or do you save it for something bigger that you really want later? Here are some tips on managing your earnings:

Save Before Spending

Before you think about spending, set aside a part of your allowance for savings. Maybe you want a new game, a bike, or you're saving up for a gift. Saving teaches you patience and planning.

Set a Budget

Think about what you need to buy each week or month. You might need to buy a snack at school or want to save for a new book. Plan how you'll use your allowance to cover these needs.

Track Your Money

Keep a record of what you earn and spend. You can use a notebook or a simple app on a device. Tracking helps you see where your money goes and can show you how fast savings can grow.

Learning the Value of Money

When you work for your money, you start to understand its value. You might begin to realize that buying a small toy every week means you can't save up for a bigger, more enjoyable item. This realization helps you make smarter choices about spending. You'll learn to ask yourself whether something is worth the money or if it's better to wait and save for something better.

Sharing and Giving

Earning money also lets you experience the joy of sharing. Maybe you decide to buy a gift for a family member's birthday, or maybe you choose to donate some of your money to help others. This part of money management is about kindness and the happiness that comes from giving.

The Big Picture

Managing chores, allowance, and spending isn't just about having a few dollars in your pocket. It's about preparing you for the bigger financial responsibilities you will face as you grow. Every dollar you save or spend teaches you about making decisions, planning ahead, and thinking about others.

This early experience with earning and managing money sets the foundation for your financial journey. As you grow, these lessons become part of a larger story of how you handle money in more complex situations.

Saving in Your Piggy Bank

When you earn money through chores and allowance, one of the smartest things you can do is start saving. A piggy bank isn't just a cute decoration for your room; it's your first bank account, where you can start building up savings for the future.

Why Save Money?

Saving money is all about planning ahead. Whether you want a new toy, a book, or you're saving up for a special gift, having savings means you can buy things when you really want them without having to ask anyone else for money. It teaches you independence and planning, and it gives you a safety net for unexpected wants or needs.

Choosing a Piggy Bank

There are all kinds of piggy banks. Some are actual pig-shaped banks, while others might look like superheroes, animals, or even treasure chests. Choose one that you like—it makes saving money more fun when you drop your coins into something that makes you smile. It doesn't matter what it looks like, as long as it helps you save.

How to Start Saving

Make It a Habit

Every time you earn money, make it a habit to put some of it into your piggy bank. It could be a few coins or a dollar each time. The amount doesn't matter as much as the act of saving regularly.

Set a Goal

Think of something you want to save for. It could be something small or something big. Having a goal makes saving more exciting because every time you add money to your piggy bank, you're getting closer to your goal.

Keep It Safe and Out of Sight

Keep your piggy bank in a safe place where you won't be tempted to take money out on a whim. Out of sight, out of mind works well here. The harder it is to access, the more likely you are to keep saving.

Watch Your Savings Grow

Every once in a while, count how much money you have saved up. This can be really exciting and motivating when you see your money pile growing. It's rewarding to see the result of your discipline and patience.

Learning to Wait

Saving money in a piggy bank teaches you about waiting and patience. When you see something you want to buy, but you know you have savings growing towards a bigger goal, you learn to think about what's more important. This skill, called delayed gratification, is very valuable as you grow older. It helps you make better choices, not just with money, but in many areas of life.

Sharing Your Savings

Sometimes, you might want to use your savings to help others. Maybe you want to buy a friend a birthday gift or help your family. Saving doesn't always have to be for yourself; it can also be about having the resources to be generous to others.

Recap

This chapter introduces the concept of money by explaining what money is and where it comes from. It explores how children can start earning their own money through chores and allowances, and it highlights the importance of beginning to save in a piggy bank.

Questions for Action:

1. What chores can you start doing to earn an allowance? Make a list and discuss it with your parents.
2. How does saving money in a piggy bank help you become more responsible with your finances?
3. Think of one thing you want to save for. How much do you need to save each week to reach your goal in a month?

Chapter 2

My Money, Your Money

Learning to Share and Spend

As you grow more comfortable with earning and saving money, the next step is learning how to share and spend it wisely. This chapter will help you understand how your decisions about money affect not just you, but also the people around you.

Understanding Sharing

Sharing money might sound a bit strange at first—after all, you've worked hard to earn and save it! But sharing doesn't just mean giving money away. It can also mean spending money on things that involve others, like buying a gift for a friend's birthday or treating your family to ice cream. When you share, you're showing that you care about others and that you understand money isn't just for personal use; it's also a way to bring joy to other people.

Why Share?

Builds Relationships

Sharing can strengthen your relationships. When you give, you're showing that you value the other person.

Teaches Gratitude

By sharing, you learn to appreciate what you have, as you see how your actions can positively impact others' lives.

Encourages Cooperation

Sharing teaches you about teamwork and how pooling resources can achieve greater things.

Smart Spending

Spending is one of the most exciting parts of having money, but it's also one of the most challenging. Smart spending means knowing how to use your money to get the most value—not just the most things.

Plan Before You Buy

Before you go to the store, think about what you need to buy. Make a list and stick to it. This helps prevent impulse buys, which are things you didn't plan to purchase and might regret later.

Compare Prices

Don't buy the first thing you see. Look around to see if another store has the same item for a cheaper price, or if there's a better alternative.

Wait on Big Purchases

If you want something expensive, wait a few days before buying it. You might find that you don't want it as much as you thought, or you might find it on sale.

Understanding Needs vs. Wants

A big part of spending wisely is understanding the difference between what you need and what you want. Needs are things that are essential, like food and a place to live. Wants are things that are nice to have but not essential, like toys and games.

Every time you think about buying something, ask yourself: Is this a need or a want? This question can help you make better choices about how to use your money.

Learning Together

Money management isn't just a solo activity; it's something you can learn with your family and friends. Discussing money decisions, like whether to buy something or save for something bigger, can help everyone learn and grow. These conversations can lead to better decisions and can teach you a lot about handling money as a team.

The Joy of Giving - Birthdays and Holidays

Giving gifts on birthdays and holidays is a tradition enjoyed around the world. It's a way to show others you care about them and are thinking about their happiness. When you give, you not only bring joy to others but also experience the pleasure of being generous.

Why Giving Feels Good

When you give someone a gift, you get to see their smile and excitement, which makes you feel good too. This feeling is known as the joy of giving. Scientists have found that giving to others can make us happier than spending money on ourselves. It strengthens our connections with others and can even make us feel like we're part of something bigger than ourselves.

Choosing the Right Gift

Listen and Observe

The best gifts are often based on what the person likes or needs. Pay attention to what your friends and family say about their hobbies, the things they like, or what they might need. This can give you great ideas for what to get them.

Make It Personal

A gift doesn't have to be expensive to be meaningful. Sometimes, a handmade card, a photo album, or even a poem can be more special than anything bought from a store. It shows you put thought and effort into their gift.

Plan Ahead

Keep a list of gift ideas and who they would be good for. When birthdays or holidays come around, you'll be prepared and won't have to rush to find something at the last minute.

Giving on a Budget

If you have your own money from allowances or chores, you might worry about how to afford gifts for everyone. Here are some tips on giving great gifts without spending a lot:

DIY Gifts

Use your skills to make something. Whether it's baking cookies, crafting a bracelet, or drawing a picture, DIY gifts are often cherished because they are one-of-a-kind and personal.

Combine Resources

If there's a more expensive gift you'd like to give, consider joining forces with siblings or friends to buy it together. This way, you can give a bigger or nicer gift without any one person bearing the full cost.

Give Experiences

Sometimes, doing something together is the best gift. Plan a day to spend with the person doing something they love, like a hike, a picnic, or a movie marathon. These memories can be more valuable than physical gifts.

The Impact of Giving

Giving teaches you about empathy and compassion. When you think about what someone else would like and go out of your way to obtain it for them, you're putting their happiness ahead of your own. This helps build strong relationships and teaches you to think about the needs and feelings of others.

Celebrating Together

Holidays and birthdays are more than just times for giving; they're also opportunities to celebrate together. These moments are chances to enjoy each other's company and appreciate the joy that comes from being part of a community, whether it's family or friends.

Understanding Needs vs. Wants

When it comes to managing money, one of the most important skills you can learn is the ability to distinguish between needs and wants. This knowledge helps you make wise decisions about how to spend your money, ensuring that you have what you need while also saving for what you truly desire.

What are Needs?

Needs are essentials, the things you must have to live safely and comfortably. They include food, shelter, clothing, and healthcare. Without these basics, it would be difficult to live a healthy life. For example, you need to eat to have energy, you need a place to live to stay safe, and you need clothes to wear for protection and warmth.

What are Wants?

Wants, on the other hand, are things that you would like to have but don't necessarily need. These can make life more enjoyable or convenient but aren't essential for your immediate survival or well-being. Wants include things like toys, video games, fashionable clothes, or the latest electronics. They are nice to have and can bring you happiness, but you can live without them if you need to.

Why is it Important to Know the Difference?

Understanding the difference between needs and wants is crucial because it helps you prioritize your spending. When you know what you truly need, you can make sure to allocate your money to those things first. This ensures that your basic requirements are taken care of before you spend money on less essential items.

How to Distinguish Between Needs and Wants

Ask Questions

When you're thinking about buying something, ask yourself a few questions:

Do I need this to live a healthy and safe life?

Can I live comfortably without it?

Is there a cheaper or free alternative that works just as well?

Create a Budget

A budget is a great tool for managing your money. It can help you set limits for your spending on both needs and wants. By seeing how much money you have and where it needs to go, you can make informed decisions about what you can afford to buy.

Prioritize Spending

Always aim to cover your needs first. Once your basic needs are met, you can use any remaining money for your wants. This might mean sometimes waiting and saving for a want, which can also make finally getting it feel even more rewarding.

The Impact of Getting it Right

By effectively managing your needs and wants, you not only ensure that you're covering your essential expenses, but you also build healthy financial habits.

This practice helps prevent unnecessary debt and stress associated with overspending on things that aren't essential. Moreover, it teaches you the value of money and the satisfaction that comes from making smart financial decisions.

Recap

This chapter covers the basics of sharing and spending wisely. It emphasizes the joy of giving during birthdays and holidays and helps kids distinguish between needs and wants.

Questions for Action:

1. Plan a gift for a friend's upcoming birthday. How will you decide what to buy within your budget?

2. List three of your recent purchases and classify them as 'needs' or 'wants'. How do these choices affect your savings?

3. How can you practice generosity within your family or community this week?

Chapter 3

The Quest for More Coins

Ways to Earn Money as a Kid

Earning money isn't just for adults. As a kid, there are plenty of creative and fun ways to earn your own cash. Whether it's to boost your savings, buy something special, or help out your family, having your own money can give you a sense of pride and independence. Here are some ideas on how you can start making money even at a young age.

Chores and Allowance

We've already talked about chores and allowance, but it's worth mentioning again because it's often the first way kids start to earn money. If you're looking for more ways to earn, consider asking your parents if there are additional chores you can take on for extra pay.

Lemonade Stand or Bake Sale

Starting a lemonade stand or a bake sale is a classic way for kids to earn money. Not only does it teach you the basics of running a business, including costs, pricing, and customer service, but it also lets you enjoy making and selling products that people love. Whether it's lemonade, cookies, or cupcakes, these sales can be a fun and profitable way to spend a sunny afternoon.

Garage Sale

If your home is cluttered with things you no longer use—like toys, books, or clothes—a garage sale might be the perfect solution. With the help of your parents, you can organize a sale and earn some money by selling items you've outgrown. It's also a great way to learn about organizing, negotiating, and handling money.

Pet Sitting and Dog Walking

For animal lovers, pet sitting or dog walking can be an enjoyable way to earn money. Many people need help with their pets when they are busy or traveling. Offering to walk dogs or look after pets in your neighbourhood can build your responsibility skills and earn you money.

Babysitting

If you're older and responsible, babysitting is a popular way to earn money. Parents often need trustworthy babysitters to look after their children. This job requires you to be very responsible, patient, and attentive, but it can be very rewarding and well-paid.

Tutoring

If you excel in a particular subject at school, consider tutoring younger students who might need help. This can be a great way to use your knowledge to help others and earn some extra cash. You can tutor subjects like math, reading, or science, or even help with homework in general.

Craft and Jewellery Making

If you're crafty, you can make and sell items like bracelets, necklaces, or handmade greeting cards. This can be a fun hobby that also earns money. You can sell your crafts to friends, family, or even online with the help of an adult.

Yard Work

Offering to do yard work like mowing lawns, raking leaves, or shovelling snow can be a good way to earn money throughout the year. Many neighbours and family friends might be glad to have the help, and it's a job that can pay well for your efforts.

Recycling

Collecting and recycling items like cans and bottles can be another way to earn money while also helping the environment. Some places offer money for recyclables, so you can turn your efforts to keep the environment clean into a profitable venture.

Using Your Talents

Think about what you're good at. Maybe you're great at making videos, drawing, or playing an instrument. You can use these skills to offer services like video editing for family events, creating artwork for friends, or playing music at local events.

Lemonade Stands and Garage Sales

When you're a kid, finding ways to make money can be part of the fun. Lemonade stands and garage sales are not only a great way to earn some cash, but they also teach valuable lessons about business and hard work. Let's explore how you can get started with these classic entrepreneurial activities.

Starting a Lemonade Stand

A lemonade stand is one of the most traditional ways for kids to earn money. It's simple to set up, but it requires planning and a bit of strategy to make it successful.

Plan Your Stand

Decide where and when you'll set up your lemonade stand. A busy location where lots of people walk by, like near a park on a sunny day, is ideal.

Weekends or after school hours are usually the best times.

Gather Supplies

You'll need lemons, sugar, water, and cups. A big pitcher for mixing your lemonade and a table to set everything up on are also essential. You might also want to create signs to attract attention and list your prices.

Make It Tasty

The better your lemonade tastes, the more likely people are to buy it and come back for more. Experiment with your recipe to find the perfect balance of sweet and tart.

Set the Right Price

Make sure your prices are reasonable so people won't hesitate to buy. A typical cup of lemonade might go for 50 cents to a dollar. If it's really hot out, you might be able to charge a bit more.

Advertise

Colourful signs can draw attention to your lemonade stand. You can also tell your friends, family, and neighbours about your stand to spread the word.

Running a Garage Sale

A garage sale is another great way for kids to earn money by selling things they no longer need. It's also an excellent opportunity to declutter your home.

Collect Items to Sell

Look around your house for toys, books, clothes, and other items you no longer use. Make sure everything is clean and in good condition.

Get Permission and Help

Ask your parents for permission and help in organizing the sale. They can assist with setting prices and deciding how to display items.

Price Items Clearly

Use stickers or tags to clearly mark prices on all items. Be realistic about pricing – remember, these are used items, and people are looking for bargains.

Advertise Your Sale

Put up signs around your neighbourhood a few days before your sale. You can also ask your parents to post about it online, like on a community Facebook page or a neighbourhood app.

Be Prepared on the Day

On the day of the sale, have a small cash box with change for customers who pay with large bills. Greet everyone who comes to look and be ready to negotiate prices – it's part of the fun and learning process!

What You Learn

Both lemonades stand and garage sales offer more than just a chance to make money. They teach you about the basics of business, like supply and demand, pricing, marketing, and customer service. These are skills that can help you in many areas of life, not just in making sales.

Being a Young Entrepreneur

Starting a business when you're young can be an exciting and rewarding experience. It's a chance to bring your ideas to life, make some money, and learn valuable skills that will serve you throughout your life. Here's how you can get started on your path as a young entrepreneur.

Find Your Idea

The first step to being a young entrepreneur is to come up with a business idea. Think about what you enjoy doing and see if there's a way to make money from it. Maybe you're good at making crafts, baking cookies, or you have a knack for fixing bikes. Or perhaps you can provide a service like tutoring, lawn mowing, or tech support for neighbours. The best business ideas come from what you know and love because that's where you'll put in your best effort.

Plan Your Business

Once you have an idea, make a simple plan. What will you sell? Who will buy it? How much will you charge? You also need to think about where you'll sell your products or services. Will you use the internet, set up a stand in your neighbourhood, or sell directly to friends and family? Planning helps you organize your thoughts and set clear goals.

Gather Resources

You might need some basic materials to get started. If you're baking, you'll need ingredients. For a service like lawn mowing, you'll need a lawnmower. Talk to your parents about what you need and see if they can help you get started. Sometimes, you can use what you already have at home to keep costs down.

Start Small

You don't need to launch a big business right away. Start small and grow gradually. For example, if you're selling handmade jewellery, start by making a few pieces and see how well they sell at a local craft fair or to people you know. Starting small lets you test out your ideas without risking a lot of money.

Market Your Business

Let people know about your business. You can make flyers, create a simple website, or use social media to spread the word (with your parents' permission and guidance). Word of mouth is also powerful, so ask your friends and family to tell others about your business.

Learn from Experience

Running your own business will teach you a lot. You'll learn how to handle money, deal with customers, and solve problems. Not everything will go perfectly, and that's okay. Each mistake is a chance to learn and improve.

Stay Committed

Being a young entrepreneur takes work. There will be challenges, but staying committed is key. Keep working towards your goals, even when it gets tough. The skills you develop by sticking with it—like determination and the ability to overcome obstacles—are just as valuable as the money you make.

Recap

Explores various ways kids can earn money beyond household chores. It discusses setting up lemonade stands, organizing garage sales, and embracing the spirit of a young entrepreneur.

Questions for Action:

1. What is one business idea you can start this season? Sketch out a simple business plan.

2. How can you make your lemonade stand or garage sale stand out? List three creative ideas.

3. Who in your life is an entrepreneur? Consider asking them for advice on starting your own small business.

Chapter 4

Guarding the Treasure Chest

Starting Your Savings Adventure

Once you've started earning money, whether from chores, a lemonade stand, or your own small business, the next crucial step is learning how to save it. Saving money is like guarding a treasure chest: it's all about keeping your coins safe for the future, whether you have a specific goal in mind or just a general idea to build a fund for later use. Here's how you can embark on your savings adventure.

Set Clear Goals

Begin by setting clear and achievable savings goals. What are you saving for? It could be a new bicycle, a video game, or even starting a college fund. When you know what you're saving for, it becomes easier to stay focused and motivated. For each goal, figure out how much money you need and how long you think it will take to save it.

Choose the Right Place to Save

Deciding where to keep your money is important. You can start with a piggy bank, but as you save more, you might want to open a savings account in a bank. Banks are safe places where your money can grow a little bit over time, thanks to interest. Interest is like a small bonus that the bank pays you for keeping your money there.

Make Saving a Habit

Make saving a regular habit. Each time you earn money, put a portion of it into your savings. A good rule of thumb is to save at least 10% of everything you earn. If you get $10, put $1 into your savings. It might not seem like much at first, but over time, it adds up.

Track Your Progress

Keep track of how much you're saving. You can use a notebook, a spreadsheet, or a savings app to help you see how close you are to reaching your goals.

Seeing the numbers grow can be exciting and encouraging.

Learn to Prioritize

Sometimes you'll have to make choices about what to spend your money on. Learning to prioritize your needs over your wants is crucial. If you spend all your money on small, less important things, you won't have enough left for the big things you really want. Always ask yourself if a purchase is worth delaying your savings goals.

Adjust as Needed

Your savings goals might change as you grow older, and that's okay. Maybe you decide you want something else more than what you were originally saving for. It's fine to adjust your goals as long as you keep the habit of saving. Just make sure to think carefully about each change and why you're making it.

Celebrate Milestones

When you reach a savings goal, celebrate your success. This doesn't mean you should spend all your savings, but acknowledging your accomplishment in some small way can be very rewarding. It encourages you to keep going and start saving for the next goal.

Goals and Wishes - Saving for Something Big

Saving money is an important skill, but it becomes especially exciting when you're saving up for something big. Whether it's a new computer, a family vacation, or even starting a college fund, having a large goal can motivate you to be more disciplined with your money. Here's how you can successfully save for your big dreams.

Define Your Big Goal

Start by clearly defining what it is you want to save for. Be as specific as possible. Instead of saying "I want to save for a new bike," find out exactly which bike you want and how much it costs. Knowing the details will help you visualize your goal more clearly and make it more tangible.

Find Out How Much You Need

Once you've decided what you're saving for, do some research to find out how much money you need to achieve your goal. Look at different stores or online to compare prices and get the best deal. This will give you a clear target to aim for.

Set a Timeline

Decide when you would like to reach your goal. Setting a deadline can help you stay on track and make consistent progress. For example, if you want to buy a $300 bike and you can save $50 a month, you'll reach your goal in six months.

Break It Down

Break your big goal into smaller, more manageable pieces. If you're saving $300, think of it as saving $50 each month, or even $12.50 each week. This makes the goal seem more achievable and less daunting.

Make a Savings Plan

Create a plan for how you will save the money. Decide how much of your allowance or earnings you will put into savings each week or month. You might need to cut back on smaller expenses or find additional ways to make money. The key is to be consistent with your savings.

Keep Your Money Safe

Decide where you will keep your savings. While a piggy bank is a good start for small amounts, consider opening a savings account for larger sums. This keeps your money safe and can also help you earn interest.

Track Your Progress

Keep track of how much money you're saving and how close you are to reaching your goal. You might want to create a chart or graph that you can update each time you save more money. Seeing the progress visually can be a huge motivator.

Stay Flexible

Sometimes, goals change or take longer to reach than you planned. That's okay. The important part is to keep saving and stay committed to your financial goals. If you encounter setbacks, adjust your plan as needed but try to keep your eye on the prize.

Celebrate Achievements

When you reach milestones along the way, celebrate your success. This doesn't mean spending your savings, but you could acknowledge your progress with a small, inexpensive reward. This keeps you motivated and makes the saving process enjoyable.

The Patience Game - Waiting for What You Want

Learning to wait for what you want is one of the most valuable skills you can develop early in life. It's often called the patience game. Whether it's saving up for a new video game or waiting for the right time to spend your hard-earned money, the ability to wait plays a crucial role in achieving your goals and managing your finances effectively.

Understanding the Value of Patience

Patience in spending and saving is about more than just biding your time. It's about understanding the right moment to act and recognizing when it's better to wait. This might mean holding off on immediate gratifications for more significant rewards in the future. Here's why patience is so important:

Avoiding Impulse Buys

Often, impulse purchases lead to regret. Something might seem like a must-have item at the moment, but after some time, its appeal can wear off. Waiting helps you figure out if your desire for a product is genuine or just a spur-of-the-moment want.

Saving for Better Things

When you practice patience, you give yourself the chance to save for high-quality items that will last longer or provide more satisfaction than cheaper, immediate buys.

Appreciating What You Get

Patience allows you to truly appreciate and value the things you work hard to obtain. When you finally achieve a goal after a period of waiting and saving, the accomplishment feels more rewarding.

Strategies for Developing Patience

Building patience might seem challenging, but there are several strategies you can employ to make it easier:

Set Clear Goals

Know exactly what you are saving for and why. This clarity makes it easier to stay focused and motivated, even when you're tempted to spend prematurely.

Create a Visual Reminder

Keep a picture of your goal item where you can see it daily, like on your bedroom wall or as a background on your phone. This reminder can help keep your focus on the prize.

Track Your Progress

Use a chart or app to track your savings progress. Seeing the visual representation of your money growing can reinforce the benefits of waiting and saving.

Practice Gratitude

Focus on what you already have, not just what you want. This mindset shift can reduce the urge to buy impulsively and increase contentment with your current possessions.

Engage in Slow Hobbies

Activities like reading, crafting, or gardening require patience and can help cultivate this skill naturally. These hobbies show that good things take time to develop and flourish.

Learning from Setbacks

Sometimes, despite your best efforts, you might dip into your savings for an unplanned expense or give in to an impulse buy. When this happens, it's important not to get discouraged. Instead, use the experience as a learning opportunity. Analyse what led to the decision and think about how you can handle similar situations in the future. Remember, developing patience is a process, and occasional setbacks are part of the journey.

The Rewards of the Patience Game

The benefits of developing patience extend beyond financial well-being. Patience helps you make more thoughtful decisions, reduces stress, and improves your interactions with others. In the realm of personal finance, it can lead to better spending habits, increased savings, and ultimately, a more secure financial future.

Recap

Focuses on saving: starting a savings adventure, setting goals for big purchases, and learning the value of patience in financial matters.

Questions for Action:

1. What is your current savings goal? Create a visual chart to track your progress.

2. Discuss with a family member about their first big savings goal. What did they learn?

3. Think of a situation where waiting helped you make a better spending decision. What happened?

Chapter 5

Money Wizards and Their Secrets

Banks: The Caves Where Money Wizards Keep Your Coins Safe

Banks play a crucial role in everyone's financial life, acting much like modern-day treasure caves where we store our money. While they might not be manned by wizards, the people who work there are experts in managing money and keeping it safe. Understanding how banks work and why they are safe places to keep your money is an important part of learning about finances.

What are Banks?

A bank is a business that deals with money. People and companies use banks to keep their money safe, to save, and to borrow more when they need it.

Banks offer various services, including savings accounts, checking accounts, loans, and mortgages. They're regulated by the government, which means they have to follow strict rules to ensure your money is safe.

Why Use a Bank?

Safety

One of the main reasons to use a bank is safety. Money kept in a bank is protected from theft, loss, and damage. Unlike keeping all your cash at home, money in the bank is safeguarded under many layers of security.

Interest

Banks pay interest on the money you save with them. Although the rates may vary and are often not very high, it's still extra money that you earn just by keeping your funds in a savings account.

Convenience

Banks offer many convenient services that make managing your money easier. You can set up automatic payments for bills, transfer money to others, and access your money from different locations through ATMs and online banking.

Record Keeping

Banks provide detailed records of your transactions, which can help you track your spending, budget better, and manage your finances. These records are also important for things like preparing taxes or getting a loan.

How Banks Keep Your Money Safe

Banks use a variety of methods to ensure that your money is safe:

Physical Security

Banks have strong vaults, security cameras, alarm systems, and guards to protect the physical building.

Insurance

In many countries, a government agency ensures the money you keep in a bank up to a certain amount. For example, in the United States, the Federal Deposit Insurance Corporation (FDIC) insures deposits up to $250,000 per depositor, per insured bank, for each account ownership category.

Cybersecurity

Banks also use advanced cybersecurity measures to protect your money from online threats. These include encryption, firewalls, and secure servers.

How to Use Banks Wisely

To make the most of what banks have to offer, consider the following tips:

Choose the Right Bank

Look for a bank that meets your needs. Consider factors like fees, interest rates, convenience, customer service, and the types of services they offer.

Understand the Fees

Banks can charge fees for various services. Understanding these fees can help you avoid unnecessary charges. For example, some banks charge for ATM use, account maintenance, and overdrawing your account.

Use Online Banking

Most banks now offer online banking, which allows you to manage your accounts from your computer or smartphone. This is a convenient way to check your balance, make transfers, and even deposit checks.

Start Saving Early

The sooner you start saving in a bank, the more you can accumulate through compound interest over time.

Interest: The Spell That Grows Your Money

Interest is like magic for your money—it has the power to make your savings grow over time without you having to do anything. Understanding how interest works is key to making the most of your savings and achieving your financial goals.

What is Interest?

Interest is essentially the cost of borrowing money or the reward for saving money. When you borrow money, you have to pay back the amount you borrowed plus an extra fee called interest. On the other hand, when you save money in a bank or invest it, you earn interest on your savings as a reward for letting the bank or investment company use your money.

How Does Interest Work?

There are two main types of interest: simple interest and compound interest.

Simple Interest

With simple interest, you earn or pay interest only on the initial amount of money you deposit or borrow. For example, if you deposit $100 in a savings account that pays 5% simple interest annually, you will earn $5 in interest each year.

Compound Interest

Compound interest is more powerful because it allows your money to grow faster over time. With compound interest, you earn interest not only on the initial amount you deposit but also on any interest you have already earned. This means your money grows exponentially. For example, if you deposit $100 in a savings account that pays 5% compound interest annually, you will earn $5 in interest the first year. In the second year, you will earn interest on both the initial $100 and the $5 you earned in interest the previous year, resulting in a higher amount of interest earned.

The Power of Compound Interest

Compound interest is often referred to as the eighth wonder of the world because of its incredible ability to grow your savings over time. The key to maximizing the power of compound interest is to start saving as early as possible and to leave your money invested for as long as possible.

Example of Compound Interest

Let's look at an example to see how compound interest can grow your savings over time:

Imagine you start saving $100 per month in a retirement account that earns an average annual return of 7%. After 30 years, you would have contributed a total of $36,000 ($100 per month for 30 years). However, thanks to compound interest, your account balance would be much higher—around $108,366! That's more than three times the amount you originally saved.

When the Money Wizard Needs Their Coins Back - Borrowing and Returning

Even the most prudent money wizards sometimes find themselves in need of extra coins. In such situations, borrowing money can be a useful tool to navigate temporary financial challenges. However, borrowing comes with responsibilities and consequences that must be carefully considered.

Understanding Borrowing

Borrowing money means taking a loan from someone else or a financial institution with the agreement to pay it back later, usually with interest.

People borrow money for various reasons, such as buying a house, paying for education, starting a business, or covering unexpected expenses.

Types of Borrowing

There are different types of borrowing options available, each with its own terms and conditions:

Personal Loans

These are loans from a bank, credit union, or online lender that can be used for various purposes. Personal loans typically have fixed monthly payments and interest rates.

Credit Cards

Credit cards allow you to borrow money up to a certain limit to make purchases. You're required to make minimum monthly payments, and interest is charged on any remaining balance.

Student Loans

These loans are specifically designed to help students pay for education expenses like tuition, books, and living expenses. They often have lower interest rates and flexible repayment options.

Mortgages

A mortgage is a loan used to buy a home. The home serves as collateral, meaning if you fail to repay the loan, the lender can take possession of the property.

Responsibilities of Borrowing

While borrowing money can provide short-term relief, it's essential to understand the responsibilities that come with it:

Repayment

Borrowers are obligated to repay the loan according to the agreed-upon terms. This includes making regular payments on time and in full.

Interest

In addition to repaying the borrowed amount, borrowers must pay interest, which is the cost of borrowing money. Interest rates can vary depending on the type of loan and the borrower's creditworthiness.

Impact on Credit

Borrowing and repaying loans can affect your credit score. Responsible borrowing and timely repayment can improve your credit score, while late or missed payments can lower it.

Risk of Default

Failing to repay a loan can have serious consequences, including damage to your credit score, legal action by the lender, and repossession of collateral (such as a home or car).

Returning the Coins

When it's time to repay a loan, it's essential to fulfil your obligations promptly and completely:

Budgeting

Make sure you budget for loan payments as part of your monthly expenses. Set aside money regularly to ensure you can meet your repayment obligations.

Prioritize Payments

If you have multiple loans, prioritize paying off high-interest debts first to minimize interest costs over time.

Communicate with Lenders

If you're experiencing financial difficulties and are unable to make payments, contact your lenders as soon as possible. They may be willing to work with you to find a solution, such as adjusting payment terms or creating a repayment plan.

Avoid Overborrowing

Only borrow what you need and can afford to repay. Avoid the temptation to borrow more than necessary, as it can lead to financial strain and difficulties in repayment.

Recap

Introduces banks as safe places to keep money, the concept of interest as a way to grow savings, and the basics of borrowing and returning money.

Questions for Action:

1. Visit a bank with a parent and learn about the different types of accounts. Which type might be right for you?

2. Calculate how much interest you could earn if you saved a certain amount of money for a year.

3. Have a discussion about borrowing: is there a time when it's okay to borrow money? What should you consider before doing so?

Chapter 6

The Marketplace Maze

Smart Shopping with Mom

The marketplace can sometimes feel like a maze, with countless products, brands, and prices vying for your attention. However, with a little guidance, you can learn to navigate this maze and become a smart shopper, making informed decisions that save you money and ensure you get the best value for your purchases.

Making a List

Before heading to the store, it's essential to make a list of the items you need to buy. This helps you stay focused and avoid impulse purchases. Sit down with your mom and discuss what you need, whether it's groceries, household items, or clothing. Write everything down to ensure you don't forget anything.

Doing Your Research

Once you have your list, it's time to do some research. Compare prices and quality of the items on your list at different stores or online retailers. Look for sales, discounts, and coupons that can help you save money. By being informed about the options available, you can make better purchasing decisions.

Setting a Budget

Before you start shopping, it's crucial to set a budget for your trip. Determine how much money you can afford to spend on each item and stick to it. This helps prevent overspending and ensures you stay within your means. If possible, involve your mom in setting the budget to get her input and guidance.

Understanding Labels and Packaging

When shopping for groceries or other items, it's essential to read labels and packaging carefully. Look for important information such as ingredients, nutritional facts, and product descriptions. This helps you make healthier choices and avoid products that may not meet your needs or preferences.

Comparing Prices

Compare prices of similar products to find the best value for your money. Look for sales, promotions, and discounts that can help you save. Keep in mind that higher prices don't always mean better quality, so it's essential to weigh the cost against the benefits of each product.

Avoiding Impulse Purchases

It's easy to get tempted by flashy displays and promotions while shopping, but it's essential to resist impulse purchases. Stick to your list and budget to avoid overspending on items you don't need. If you see something you want but didn't plan to buy, take a moment to think it over before making a decision.

Checking Reviews and Recommendations

Before making a purchase, consider checking online reviews and recommendations from other shoppers. This can provide valuable insights into the quality and performance of products you're considering. Look for reviews from reputable sources and consider both positive and negative feedback.

Being Mindful of Sales Tactics

Be aware of sales tactics used by retailers to encourage spending, such as limited-time offers, buy-one-get-one-free deals, and upselling. While these tactics can be tempting, it's essential to evaluate whether the offer is truly beneficial to you and fits within your budget.

Coupons and Sales - The Quest for Bargains

In the quest for bargains, coupons and sales are powerful tools that can help you save money on your purchases. Whether you're shopping for groceries, clothing, or household items, knowing how to find and use coupons effectively can make a significant difference in your overall spending. Let's delve into the world of coupons and sales to understand how they work and how you can maximize your savings.

Understanding Coupons

Coupons are vouchers or codes that offer discounts or special deals on specific products or services. They can be found in various forms, including paper coupons, digital coupons, and promotional codes. Coupons typically offer a percentage off the regular price, a specific dollar amount discount, or a buy-one-get-one-free deal.

Where to Find Coupons

Coupons can be found in a variety of places, both online and offline:

Newspapers and Magazines

Many newspapers and magazines include coupon inserts or special sections with money-saving offers.

Online Coupon Websites

There are numerous websites dedicated to offering coupons for various products and retailers. You can search for coupons by product category or specific brands.

Store Websites and Apps

Some retailers offer digital coupons that you can clip or download directly from their websites or mobile apps.

Manufacturer Websites

Many manufacturers offer coupons on their websites for their products. You can often find printable coupons or digital coupons that you can use in stores.

Store Loyalty Programs

Some stores have loyalty programs that offer exclusive discounts and coupons to members.

Tips for Using Coupons Effectively

To make the most of coupons and maximize your savings, consider the following tips:

Check Expiration Dates

Be mindful of coupon expiration dates and use them before they expire to avoid missing out on savings.

Combine Coupons with Sales

Look for opportunities to combine coupons with store sales or promotions for even greater savings. This can result in significant discounts on your purchases.

Read the Fine Print

Pay attention to the terms and conditions of each coupon, including any restrictions or limitations. Some coupons may only be valid for certain products or have minimum purchase requirements.

Plan Your Shopping Trips

Plan your shopping trips around coupon availability and store promotions to take full advantage of the savings opportunities.

Understanding Sales

Sales are promotional events during which retailers offer discounts on their products or services. Sales can occur for various reasons, such as holidays, clearance events, or to attract customers during slower periods. During sales, prices are typically reduced temporarily, allowing shoppers to purchase items at a lower cost.

Tips for Shopping Sales

To make the most of sales and maximize your savings, consider the following tips:

Research Sale Events

Stay informed about upcoming sales events at your favourite retailers by checking their websites, newsletters, or social media pages.

Compare Prices

Before making a purchase during a sale, compare prices at different retailers to ensure you're getting the best deal.

Shop Early

During popular sales events, such as Black Friday or Cyber Monday, popular items may sell out quickly. Shop early to avoid missing out on the best deals.

Set a Budget

Even during sales, it's essential to stick to your budget to avoid overspending. Determine how much you can afford to spend and prioritize your purchases accordingly.

The Enchanted Objects - Advertising and Its Tricks

Advertising has a magical way of making ordinary objects seem extraordinary. From shiny new gadgets to mouth watering food, advertisements have the power to captivate our attention and persuade us to buy things we may not even need. But behind the enchanting facade lies a world of clever tricks and strategies designed to influence our buying decisions.

Appealing Imagery

Advertisers use captivating images and visuals to grab our attention and create desire for their products. Whether it's a beautiful model wearing the latest fashion or a delicious-looking meal, these images trigger our emotions and make us want to experience the same feelings associated with the product.

Persuasive Language

Advertisements often use persuasive language to convince us that their product is the best choice. They may use words like "amazing," "revolutionary," or "must-have" to create a sense of urgency and importance around their product.

Social Proof

Many advertisements use social proof to make their products seem more desirable. This could be in the form of celebrity endorsements, customer testimonials, or positive reviews. When we see others enjoying a product, we're more likely to want it too.

Limited Time Offers

Scarcity is a powerful motivator, and advertisers often use limited-time offers and promotions to create a sense of urgency. Whether it's a "sale ends soon" message or a "limited edition" product, these tactics make us feel like we need to act quickly to avoid missing out.

Subliminal Messaging

Advertisements sometimes use subtle cues and symbols to influence our subconscious minds. These could be hidden messages or images that trigger certain emotions or desires without us even realizing it.

Recap

Teaches kids about smart shopping practices, using coupons and looking for sales, and understanding the influence of advertising.

Questions for Action:

1. Next time you go shopping, help your parent find and use at least one coupon.

2. Make a list of advertisements you see in one day. Do they make you want to buy things you don't need?

3. Discuss with a friend or family member about the last time they made a purchase because of an ad. What was the outcome?

Chapter 7

The Treasure Map Redrawn

Budgeting: Planning Your Spending Adventure

Budgeting is like creating a map for your financial journey, helping you plan and manage your money wisely. It involves setting limits on how much you'll spend on different expenses, such as groceries, entertainment, and savings, to ensure you're not spending more than you earn. Let's explore how budgeting can help you navigate your spending adventure.

Setting Goals

The first step in budgeting is to identify your financial goals. Whether it's saving for a vacation, buying a new gadget, or building an emergency fund, having clear goals will guide your budgeting decisions and motivate you to stick to your plan.

Tracking Income and Expenses

To create a budget, you need to know how much money you're earning and where it's going. Keep track of your income from sources like allowances, part-time jobs, or gifts, as well as your expenses on things like food, transportation, and entertainment.

Allocating Funds

Once you know how much money you have coming in and going out, it's time to allocate funds to different categories based on your priorities. Start by covering essential expenses like rent and utilities, then allocate money for savings goals and discretionary spending.

Prioritizing Needs vs. Wants

Budgeting helps you distinguish between needs and wants, ensuring you prioritize spending on necessities while still allowing for some discretionary spending on things you enjoy. This can help you avoid overspending and ensure you're putting your money where it matters most.

Adjusting as Needed

Your budget isn't set in stone—it's a flexible tool that can be adjusted as your circumstances change. If you encounter unexpected expenses or your income changes, be prepared to reassess your budget and make adjustments to ensure it remains realistic and achievable.

The Four Coin Jars - Save, Spend, Donate, Invest

Managing money wisely involves more than just earning and spending—it's about allocating your resources effectively to achieve your financial goals. The concept of the four-coin jars—save, spend, donate, and invest—provides a simple framework for organizing your finances and ensuring you're using your money in ways that align with your values and priorities.

Save Jar

The save jar is like a piggy bank for your future goals and emergencies. It's where you set aside money for long-term objectives, such as buying a car, going to college, or building an emergency fund. Saving money allows you to prepare for the unexpected and work towards your dreams without relying on debt. By regularly contributing to your save jar, even small amounts, you can gradually build a nest egg that provides financial security and peace of mind.

Spend Jar

The spend jar is for covering your everyday expenses and discretionary purchases. It's where you allocate money for things like groceries, entertainment, clothing, and dining out. The spend jar helps you prioritize your spending and ensure you're living within your means. By tracking your expenses and sticking to a budget, you can make informed decisions about where your money goes and avoid overspending on unnecessary items.

Donate Jar

The donate jar is for giving back to others and supporting causes you care about. It's where you set aside money for charitable donations, volunteer activities, or random acts of kindness. Giving to others not only helps those in need but also brings joy and fulfillment to your own life. Whether you're donating to a local charity, supporting a crowdfunding campaign, or helping a friend in need, the donate jar allows you to make a positive impact on the world around you.

Invest Jar

The invest jar is for growing your wealth and securing your financial future. It's where you allocate money for long-term investments, such as stocks, bonds, mutual funds, or real estate. Investing allows your money to work for you, generating returns and building wealth over time. Whether you're saving for retirement, planning for your children's education, or aiming for financial independence, the invest jar is an essential tool for achieving your long-term financial goals.

Keeping Track of Your Coins

Once you've allocated your money to the four-coin jars, it's essential to keep track of your coins to ensure you're staying on track with your financial plan. This involves regularly monitoring your income, expenses, savings, and investments to ensure they align with your goals and priorities.

There are various tools and methods you can use to keep track of your coins, such as:

Budgeting Apps

There are many budgeting apps available that can help you track your income and expenses, set savings goals, and monitor your progress over time. These apps often sync with your bank accounts and credit cards, making it easy to see where your money is going.

Spreadsheets

Creating a simple spreadsheet to track your income, expenses, savings, and investments can be an effective way to stay organized and monitor your financial progress. You can customize the spreadsheet to fit your needs and update it regularly to reflect changes in your financial situation.

Regular Check-Ins

Set aside time each month to review your financial situation and make any necessary adjustments to your budget or investment strategy. This allows you to stay proactive and make informed decisions about your money.

Recap

Focuses on budgeting, using a four-jar system to manage money (save, spend, donate, invest), and keeping track of finances.

Questions for Action:

1. Design your own budget using the four-jar system. How much of your money will you put in each jar?

2. Keep a spending diary for a week. What insights do you gain about your spending habits?

3. Plan a small donation to a cause you care about. How does it feel to use your money to help others?

Chapter 8

The Future Treasure Hunt

Dreams of the Future - Why It's Never Too Early to Save

The future is like a treasure waiting to be discovered, full of endless possibilities and opportunities. Whether you dream of traveling the world, starting your own business, or buying your dream home, saving money is the key to turning those dreams into reality. Here's why it's never too early to start saving for the future.

1. Building Financial Security

Saving money provides a safety net that can protect you from unexpected expenses or financial emergencies. By setting aside money in a savings account or emergency fund, you can have peace of mind knowing that you're prepared for whatever the future may hold. Whether it's a car repair, medical bill, or job loss, having savings allows you to navigate life's challenges without relying on credit cards or loans.

2. Achieving Your Goals

Saving money is essential for achieving your long-term goals and aspirations. Whether you dream of buying a house, going to college, or retiring comfortably, saving money allows you to make progress towards those goals over time. By setting specific savings targets and regularly contributing to your savings accounts, you can steadily work towards turning your dreams into reality.

3. Taking Advantage of Opportunities

Saving money gives you the flexibility and freedom to take advantage of opportunities when they arise. Whether it's investing in a promising business venture, seizing a once-in-a-lifetime travel opportunity, or pursuing further education, having savings allows you to say "yes" to opportunities that can enrich your life and broaden your horizons.

4. Harnessing the Power of Compound Interest

The earlier you start saving, the more time your money has to grow through the power of compound interest. Compound interest allows your savings to generate earnings, which are then reinvested to generate even more earnings over time. By starting to save early, you can harness the full potential of compound interest and significantly increase the size of your nest egg by the time you reach your goals.

Planting the Seeds - Investing in Your Future

Investing in your future is like planting seeds in a garden, nurturing them with care and patience until they grow into strong and fruitful trees. Whether you're saving for retirement, building wealth, or achieving financial independence, investing is essential for securing your financial future. Here's why planting the seeds of investment is crucial for long-term success.

1. Building Wealth Over Time

Investing allows your money to work for you, generating returns and growing over time. By investing in assets like stocks, bonds, mutual funds, or real estate, you have the potential to earn higher returns than you would with traditional savings accounts or certificates of deposit. Over the long term, the power of compounding can significantly increase the size of your investment portfolio and help you build wealth for the future.

2. Beating Inflation

Inflation erodes the purchasing power of your money over time, making it essential to invest in assets that can outpace inflation and preserve the value of your savings. Historically, stocks and other growth-oriented investments have provided returns that exceed the rate of inflation, allowing investors to maintain and even increase their purchasing power over time.

3. Diversifying Your Portfolio

Investing allows you to diversify your portfolio, spreading your risk across different asset classes and investments. By diversifying, you can reduce the impact of market fluctuations and minimize the risk of significant losses. A well-diversified portfolio includes a mix of stocks, bonds, real estate, and other assets that perform differently under various market conditions.

4. Achieving Financial Goals

Investing is essential for achieving your long-term financial goals, such as buying a house, sending your children to college, or retiring comfortably. By investing regularly and staying committed to your investment plan, you can make steady progress towards your goals and secure a brighter financial future for yourself and your family.

Sharing the Wealth - Why Giving Can Make You Happy

Sharing the wealth is about more than just accumulating money—it's about using your resources to make a positive impact on the lives of others and the world around you. Whether through charitable donations, volunteer work, or acts of kindness, giving back can bring joy and fulfillment to your own life. Here's why sharing the wealth can make you happy.

1. Making a Difference

Giving back allows you to make a meaningful difference in the lives of others, whether it's supporting a cause you care about, helping those in need, or contributing to your community. Knowing that your actions have a positive impact can bring a sense of fulfillment and purpose to your life.

2. Cultivating Gratitude

Giving back can cultivate feelings of gratitude and appreciation for what you have. By helping those less fortunate, you gain a greater appreciation for the blessings in your own life and develop a deeper sense of empathy and compassion for others.

3. Strengthening Relationships

Giving back can strengthen your relationships with others, whether it's bonding with friends and family over shared experiences or connecting with like-minded individuals through volunteer work or charitable organizations. Shared acts of kindness and generosity can create lasting bonds and foster a sense of community and belonging.

4. Enhancing Well-Being

Numerous studies have shown that giving back is linked to improved mental and emotional well-being. Helping others can boost your mood, reduce stress, and increase feelings of happiness and satisfaction. The act of giving activates regions of the brain associated with pleasure and reward, leading to a "helper's high" that leaves you feeling uplifted and fulfilled.

Recap

Encourages thinking about long-term financial goals, the basics of investing, and the benefits of sharing wealth.

Questions for Action:

1. With a parent, research a type of investment suitable for young people. What are the risks and rewards?

2. Imagine your future self in 10 years. What financial state do you hope to be in?

3. Discuss with your family about the importance of giving back. How might you incorporate giving into your future financial plans?

Conclusion

Looking ahead, the adventures we've embarked on are just the beginning. With a solid foundation in financial literacy, you're now better prepared to face new challenges and seize opportunities that come your way. Whether it's saving for college, investing in your first business, or planning for long-term goals like retirement, the tools and knowledge you've gained will guide you. Staying informed, continually learning, and adapting to new financial landscapes will help you maintain control of your financial destiny.

Moreover, true success in managing money isn't just measured by the balance in your bank account, but by achieving personal bliss—a life well-saved that aligns with your deepest values and aspirations. This means finding a balance between saving for the future and enjoying the present, investing in experiences that enrich your life, and using your financial resources to enhance your happiness and well-being. The ultimate reward of being a young money master is the freedom and peace of mind to live a fulfilling life, rich in experiences and shared with people you care about.

As we close this chapter, remember that the journey to financial mastery is ongoing. The seas of finance are vast and full of both challenges and opportunities. By continuing to apply what you've learned, staying curious, and embracing new experiences, you'll navigate these waters successfully. So, here's to your future—a future where you are not only a master of your finances but also a creator of a life filled with joy, purpose, and prosperity. Let this book be a compass that helps guide your way as you continue to explore, grow, and achieve your financial goals.

However, the journey doesn't have to be a solitary one. Joining a community of like-minded individuals can greatly enhance your learning and offer support as you apply these principles in real life. Here are a few ways you can connect with our community and continue your journey toward financial empowerment:

Follow Us on Social Media

Stay updated with the latest tips, success stories, and motivational content by following our social media pages. It's a perfect way to stay engaged and inspired on your financial journey.

Explore Our Websites

For more in-depth resources, personal stories, and educational content, visit our websites at Dove V. Weaver for personal branding insights and Closer To Our Dreams for broader business perspectives and resources. These platforms are designed to support you as you grow and learn.

Join Our 30-Day Manifest Your Dreams Challenge!

Are you ready to transform your life and manifest your deepest dreams? We are thrilled to invite you to our **30-Day Manifest Your Dreams Challenge** on Facebook! This challenge is designed to guide you through a transformative journey, helping you achieve your goals and unlock your full potential.

🔗 Join the Challenge Now!

Here's what you can expect from this life-changing challenge:

- **Daily Inspirational Prompts:** Each day, you'll receive powerful prompts to keep you motivated and focused on your dreams.
- **Expert Guidance:** Gain insights from experts who will share their wisdom on manifesting and achieving goals.
- **Supportive Community:** Connect with like-minded individuals who are on the same journey, providing encouragement and support.

- **Transformative Exercises:** Engage in exercises that will help you align your thoughts and actions with your dreams.

Don't miss this opportunity to make your dreams a reality. Click the link above and join our vibrant community of dreamers and achievers. Your journey to a fulfilled and empowered life starts now!

We can't wait to see you there!

Warm regards,

By participating in this challenge, you'll not only set the stage for personal growth but also inspire others in the community to reach for their dreams. Let's embark on this incredible journey together!

Join the Challenge Now!

🌟 Manifest your dreams, transform your life! 🌟

We believe that every individual has the potential to achieve their dreams with the right knowledge and a supportive community. By connecting with us, you're taking an active step towards not just understanding money, but mastering it in a way that aligns with your personal and entrepreneurial dreams.

Remember, every big achievement begins with the decision to try. Join us today, and let's make those dreams a reality!

"Help Spread the Word - Support Our Mission!"

As you've reached the end of this book, we hope you've been inspired, educated, and empowered to make a positive impact in your community. We're grateful for your support and would like to ask for your help in spreading our message even further.

Your Donation Matters

Your contribution will enable us to:

- Reach more readers with our book
- Create more resources and content to support our mission
- Build a community of like-minded individuals who share our values

Every Amount Counts

Whether you can give $5, $10, or $50, every donation brings us closer to achieving our goals. Your support is a vote of confidence in our work and will help us continue to make a difference.

How to Donate

You can donate here

Dovev Weaver

Scan to pay $Coachdtalks

Thank You!

From the bottom of our hearts, thank you for considering a donation. Your support means the world to us and will help us continue to inspire and empower others.

www.ingramcontent.com/pod-product-compliance
Lightning Source LLC
LaVergne TN
LVHW022007200926
848481LV00007B/2272